I HOPE SHE FINDS THIS

Also by r.h. Sin

I HOPE SHE FINDS THIS

r.h. Sin

Andrews McMeel
PUBLISHING®

INCIPIT

Where it begins.

They say love hurts, but what they don't tell you is that, for most of your life, you will be taught lessons in love from people incapable of loving you properly—relationship after relationship, a tragic chain of emotional anguish and disappointment. Your first relationship will likely stem from the neglect caused by those in your home, and so you will then embark on this journey to fill the void left by your family. Young, vulnerable and naive, sad and a little broken, one by one, the wolves in search of sheep will use the word "love" as a tool of manipulation. You'll struggle through those relationships; you'll lose so much of yourself during those moments, and although you'll survive, your definition of love will be altered, fractured by individuals who never intended to love you in the way you needed.

I wish I had better examples of what love should be or could be. So much of the chaos one witnesses as a child, storms created by the elders, normalize a destructive version of what a relationship consists of—the screaming and yelling, a fog of tension filling each room. Fires made to burn, transforming everyday moments to ash. With all the flames burning, you'd think that it would be easy to keep warm, but, too often, I found winter during summer, witnessing my parents grow cold toward one another.

From a very young age and those examples set before you by family, you learn that love is about enduring others or that you must fight each day to survive it. What I mean by this is that, right now, you're probably in a relationship with someone who forces you to struggle from one end of the day down to the last moments of the night. You're not thriving in that space; you endure, but, even then, your heart is fed up with fighting and feeling like it has to go to war when love should be about peace.

In my own life, I have found myself at war while claiming to be in love. Often, I have found myself in a fight for peace while trying to maintain a relationship with someone who only intends to fight against the ideas of everything I've been working toward—planting seeds of hope in tainted soil, thinking that I could grow in a space without being nurtured. I sought out companionship and found nothing but resentment and regret. That desire to be loved drives the heart into hands that are not fit to hold it, and once we're there in that pit of hell that disguised itself as a relationship, we're conflicted because we've developed genuine feelings for a person incapable of feeling the same way. And that person often represents a toxic example of love.

If love is kind, then why is there no compassion? If love is strength, then why must the heart feel weak whenever in that person's presence? We are continually learning about love from people who don't love us. And maybe this is why you feel like you can't let go; somewhere along the way, you stopped believing in true love because the " love" you've received has always been fraudulent. It's hard to believe in something you've never witnessed; it's challenging to hold out hope for something that has always been too late to arrive or hasn't shown itself at all.

You often question your self-worth, or maybe you've struggled with self-love. And, sometimes, you choose the person you love over yourself, despite the pain they've caused inside your heart. You've even gone as far as to think of yourself as weak due to your struggles with moving on. I, for one, believe that you're strong enough to endure, and so that's what you do, but if you're strong enough to deal with the pain, you are also strong enough to face the pain in letting go. It's time to get back to doing what makes you happy instead of choosing to endure a relationship that causes your heart to feel sad. It's going to take some time; you're going to struggle because your feelings for this person are genuine, despite their inability to match your efforts. Of course, it's easier said than done, but you must love yourself enough to break free from this prison of heartache. You have overcome so much in your life, and you are a survivor of many things. It's time to fully live in the love you are capable of creating for yourself. It's time to see the gift of being alone and detaching from the person who makes you feel lonely. The absence of someone who hurts you provides you with an opportunity to make room for the one who will love you the way you need. More than ever, and through all of this, you must master the ability to turn your love inward. It would be best if you gave yourself all the things you've provided to the people who didn't honestly care.

Parallel.

Foolish of me to think about you; selfish of me to want to meet
you only when the person I'm with withholds their affections.
And, let's be honest, you're probably doing the same thing as me,
wasting your time on something temporary while daydreaming
about the evenings we could have. One moment, you're in love;
the next, you're in hell, waiting for another moment of joy, hoping
for something good to happen, and, somewhere amid the fog, you
picture me in a wooden frame. There's another photo hanging next
to it: you, finally happy, smiling in my arms. You don't stay there
long enough because you find yourself back on that emotional
roller coaster with the person you wish were me, and I do the same.
Maybe this is why we can't find one another, stuck on lovers who
don't love us. Saying that we deserve better, but we don't act like it.

Below, above.

I mourned you, and even then, I couldn't leave. Once alive, nearly ghostlike, our love became haunting. It ended way before any of us walked away; we just lingered near this pit in the ground, afraid to bury whatever was left—avoiding the truth of it being over.

One ending.

We treat relationships like lifelines, bridging ourselves to others as if they will always lend us the ability to travel over raging waters while searching for peace. Strangers become lovers, and, with love, they feel like a version of family or even a home. We tear down our walls to allow them to evolve into the foundation that is our life, and when it all begins to crumble, we feel the earth shake beneath our feet, but the ending is never permanent. You see, for a time, whatever was shared can feel like everything we could ever want until we figure out that the person we love is incapable of being all that we need. When it ends, the feeling is as if we've been gut punched and all the air has been ripped from our lungs. But, not too long after, you find out that you can breathe again, and a life built around the person you love can be rebuilt in their absence. With time, you discover that the ending of a relationship gives life to infinite possibilities, some of which can lead you back to yourself and further away from the things that make you unhappy. The ending of one relationship gives way to an invitation to self-love. And maybe each relationship is some lifeline, bridging us to different realities—some where dreams come true and others where nightmares come to life—but even when those lines are severed, you can still create new connections.

They return.

You asked me why they come back, and maybe the answer is as simple as because they believe that you'll let them back in, despite all the lying and betrayal. You see, there's nothing nice about it, nothing to romanticize. There's nothing beautiful about the fact that the person who made you feel ugly inside wants another opportunity to hurt you the same way as before. Logically, you shouldn't be happy about the return of someone who made you feel sad, but, somewhere within your heartache, you fool yourself into believing that it can all be better at a different time, maybe another place. The problem has been that you see this particular person as "the one" when, in all honesty, they're just the one keeping you from walking toward a future that is filled with the love you claim to want. And the problem with placing great expectations on someone who is incapable of living up to those ideas is that it is not always clear that you are trying to build a future with someone better off in your past. I can understand the pain of losing the person you genuinely care about, but it just so happens that there will come a time where you will see the joy in refusing to allow that person back into your life.

The exes always come back because they think they can, and often they arrive with the same bullshit as before. You've seen that movie; you know the way it ends, and it's time to rewrite the script or, better yet, create an entirely new one, something worthy of being entertained.

500 days of.

tired of missing things
that no longer belong to me
now dealing with the heartbreaking task
of figuring out what's wrong with me

i was never okay; nothing was fine
now that i can admit
this relationship felt like death
and all this time, i wanted to live

my heart was your doormat
and my soul almost the same
i'd be giving you the power
if it was you i decided to blame

but i always knew, the suspicion grew
with every waking moment
most of this was my choosing
i'll stand right here and own it

i expected more from a person
committed to doing less
i decided to try harder
for someone who
was never worth my best

love can be cruel and painful
but only if you let it be
i took the pain you gave me
and became strong enough
to set myself free

it was i alone; you never deserved the credit
i had my expectations, my standards
you never met them

i mourned us every morning
and by night, i was restless
this emotional war
left me battle-tested

til one day, it made sense
I finally knew what I needed to do
was to accept that it was never me
and that the problem was always you

Lost, not found.

You always find your way back to me, like the ocean returning to itself. And each time you're at my door, you're a bit more broken than before. Where were you all this time? Where do you go when you leave? Where do you travel when you walk in the direction opposite of me? It's like I've become medicine, a cure for the moment, and when you feel better, you leave in search of something better, only to discover more hurt and anguish. You'll eventually realize that I'd been best for you, but I'll be gone, so far gone from any way of being found.

This absence.

The less you were around, the better I felt. I didn't realize this until it was nearly over. And maybe that's what helps me sleep at night. Knowing that the loss wasn't you; it was my peace of mind. The gift of joy is your replacement.

Silent suffering.

You're the suffer-in-silence type. You claim to be okay, despite a
continuous waterfall of sadness flowing down the sides of your
heart. You smile amid emotional turbulence because you refuse
to let others see you breaking, but I want you to know that those
fractures you've hidden have meaning and that pain you feel is not
something to be ashamed of. You don't have to do this alone; you
don't have to bury your heartache out of fear of being a burden to
others. You've turned your back on what you've been feeling, and
now it's time to face your truth.

You're still dealing with a lot of fucked-up shit that you haven't
talked about because you don't want to be judged by the people
around you. So much of what you don't say continuously keeps
you up at night as your mind plays out different scenarios of what
could happen. You lose sleep over all the feelings you push down,
and every time you think you've escaped those emotional truths,
they haunt you in the form of nightmares. It hasn't been easy; this
road has been rough, and there have been several times when you
felt like you wouldn't be able to go on. The pain lingers when you
ignore it. See yourself; see your truth.

If breaking your heart doesn't hurt him, he doesn't love you. A man who genuinely cares for your heart feels pain in his whenever he lets you down.

Something to cling to.

You may question why you were so willing to give your heart to the wrong person. Maybe it was the fact that you've been struggling with your anxiety; it could also have been the depression you've faced. The heartache and the troubles of losing anyone can cause this crippling feeling of neglect and abandonment. And so, the first person to make you feel anything good is the one you fall for instantly. It just so happens that not everyone who makes you feel loved intends to love you the way you've hoped.

_____

I get it; seeking out help is difficult when you don't even know what the hell is going on in your heart. It's so fucking hard to explain what you feel when you can't pull the words from your soul.

Fear of lonely.

There's a form of loneliness so painful that it makes you miss people, even the ones who hurt you the most. Your exes know this, and they will often attempt to reenter your life by way of your fear of being alone. Don't let the feelings of loneliness drive you back into the arms of people who only intend to hurt you again.

Wait for morning.

Midnight always arrived with reminders of how lonely I'd been; the weekends made it even worse. Those hours when you can't sleep after a day filled with gloom feels like hell. With no one to talk to, the night drags on like a car without wheels. You just lie there, eyes fixed on the ceiling, noticing the lines where the paint has begun to chip as you wait for the sun to show its face so that you can try to survive another day without anyone to share it with.

Our youth.

How sad that we destroy all means of happiness in our youth to entertain dead-end relationships filled with empty promises instead of leaning more into ourselves with the love we've wasted on others. I sometimes wish I had another chance to get love myself from the start before I'd ever chosen to invest my energy in people who would only take without giving anything in return.

All but silent.

Love letters become ransom notes; relationships crumble into prisons. Presently, I wish placing you in my past was as easy as dreaming up our future with no real foundation to stand on or proof that this would otherwise turn out well. My heart first swelled full of love, then sometime later, due to the abuse it took from your hands. I used to be anxious to see you, but that anxiety now mirrors the negative tension you cause whenever we're together. Look how far we've come, to an end with nothing left to give one another but silence.

———————————————

This night had no moon; ironically, no one saw the sun that day in my city because the clouds masked the sunshine. All the things that should be where they should be are missing. Just like you were supposed to be here, but you're not. And so I sit in the dark with a mental list of all my regrets, searching for a way out of loving you.

The longer it goes on, the further your heart sinks, deeper into a place of confusion. You develop a kind of mistrust for yourself. On the one hand, you want love; on the other, you feel stuck between moving forward and scared about what you'll be leaving behind. You lose nothing when you walk away from the wrong person, but the problem is you believe that, despite all the pain they've caused you, something will one day go right, and they'll be willing to make changes based upon the effort you make. More often than not, the energy given to the wrong person is never fully realized and does nothing to reinforce change. In simplest terms, someone who doesn't genuinely care about you will never appreciate the love you give them. And so, despite how difficult it may be, you must find the strength to move on. You must find the courage to walk away so that you can be closer to everything you deserve. I know you don't know me, and maybe this message is too hard to accept, but, all in all, I hope it reaches you. I hope this inspires you at this moment. Thank you for being so strong.

I don't dream in color as much as I used to; these monochrome nightmares, like something out of the '50s, stick with me like the sun during daylight. I'm restless when I don't want to be, afraid to sleep—scared to stare into the mirror, fearful of what I'll see.

We're masterful in our molding of the past, restructuring the ugliest of moments to be beautiful. Afraid to find reasons to leave, we stretch the truth, avoiding the lies.

I wanted to sleep; I didn't want to face the agony. I had no desire to feel or think about what happened, but even then, I knew that if I closed my eyes, I'd find remnants of you lurking around in my nightmares. Crumbs from every lie told. Fragments of my heart scattered across every inch of this room from every step I tried to take toward the exit after you broke my fucking heart. I wanted to sleep, but I'll do this instead. Write down every painful word in hopes of it resonating with the person who finds this; maybe then I'll no longer feel alone.

There will come a time when all you wish to do is cry, but even as that ocean of emotion attempts to flood the shore, those rain clouds in your heart will refuse to pour. You'll sit there alone in that dark room, tossing and turning in silence. Your heart will race in a way that feels like violence.

You are magic, but none of it will change him. Your magic was always meant to save yourself. So, leave.

Maybe we do have the wrong timing, or perhaps we weren't meant
to be with one another. You keep saying, "Maybe next time,"
but with time, I'm sure I will have found someone willing to be
everything you refuse to be right now.

There's a physically felt sadness, and when it comes, it leaves you forever changed.

———————————————

I have always struggled with telling people how I feel because I never want my sadness to be a burden. And maybe this is why I've held on to the fractured parts of myself for so long, afraid that heartache would weigh you down or push you out of my life.

some of the solitude
is heaven some of the time
but to be alone and lonely
is hell on earth

I try this inner talk thing now and then; it's more like begging, I guess. Pleading with my mind to please stop the madness. Please stop overthinking when I should be asleep. Restless over scenarios of what could have happened while painting over what actually happened. Sometimes it feels like I'm at war with myself in my search for peace.

The rain sounds different when your heart is breaking. It's like each drop sings its own melody, all of it melancholy blue.

Talking to myself because I know that if I'm not able to comprehend my own feelings, how will you? But you're here now, your eyes scanning from left to right on this page, and I'm asking you, "What is it that I'm feeling?" Can you tell me? Do you know this type of loneliness, the kind where you're not alone but you feel like you have no one or nothing? Do you know how it feels to experience pain but not be able to locate the wound? Or when your heart is so broken that you discover the sound of silence? You hear what people aren't saying; you see things believed to be invisible and yet with this newfound ability to recognize the sorrow surrounding you. There's still difficulty putting words to what you're feeling, and that itself hurts.

The day you decide to let go of the people who hurt you is the moment you discover that it's the ones closest to you breaking your heart. Your refusal to entertain toxic relationships will push you to the peak of loneliness until you find out that sometimes being alone is a gift.

I, myself, have lost the bulk of my family due to their inability to treat me as such, and most of my relationships have gone to hell because those I'd chosen to be with decided it best to torch my dreams of peace and happiness.

A guideline.

Don't let your past dictate your future. Don't allow what you're used to, in an effort to prevent you from having what you deserve. Our past relationships often mold our perception of what a relationship consists of. You're so used to being hurt that you have the urge to run away when things are "too good" simply because it's unfamiliar, but sometimes unfamiliarity can breed success. Remember those who have hurt you; use those people as guidelines and examples of who to avoid. Life's too short to be unhappy.

A change will come.

When I was living in the moments of being lied to and cheated on, I questioned myself. I wondered how someone I truly cared about could even hurt me like that, but the funny thing is, I'm now thankful for the pain and the lessons I learned. Amazing how that pain can lead you on a path to something greater. We struggle to hold on to something that doesn't deserve our energy, but the pain influences change. You reach a breaking point, and the strength you used to hold on to becomes the strength that enables you to let go. In so many ways, the person who mistreats you is doing you a favor, merely pushing you into a better direction and or the arms of someone better. I know for a fact that there's life after heartache, and the fact that your relationship failed is proof that there's something more out there for you. Things do get better.

holding on to what we had
yet claiming to let go of the past
i'm good, i'm fine,
i'm okay, when they ask
searching for forever, but i'm lost, it never lasts
starting with someone new
i must do the hardest task
discovering something new, but old memories
float to surface
afraid to trust again
this type of feeling
makes me nervous

Healing begins when you sever ties with people who are responsible for your scars.

See that there is true love waiting for you within your own skin.

it's beautiful
the way you know when
to be the storm or the shelter

There will come a time when you'll get sick of waiting and you'll discover the cure of letting go.

some will feel like home
and others will resemble hell

Listen to her silence. This is when she'll say the most.

Overthinking weighs heavily on the mind in search of rest.

_____

went searching for love
got lost in lies

this was far from giving up
this was a woman tired
of the bullshit
and finding the courage
to leave your ass behind

Mistake not.

We're human. No one is perfect, and I don't think women expect
men to be without flaws, but mistakes and choices are not one and
the same when it comes to disloyalty. If you have to hide something
from the one who loves you, then, in all honesty, you know it's
wrong, but you choose to go through with it anyway. Your only
mistake is thinking she'll never find out. You only apologize after
she realizes what you've done; you're only sorry because you got
caught, and even then, "I'm sorry" isn't enough because a woman
knows that if she'd never found out, you'd most likely continue
to do what you've kept in the dark. Choosing to be disloyal to
someone who remains by your side is the easiest way to play
yourself and lose something that is most valuable—a good woman.
This is a life lesson, something always to remember. Think before
you act; avoid actions that would undermine the way she feels
about you.

She keeps things to herself out of fear of being judged. She notices
things but remains quiet in an attempt to avoid an argument. She
feels so much pain but still finds the strength to smile. She claims
to be okay because she doesn't want to annoy others with her
issues. She's mean and sometimes cold because she knows how
it feels to be hurt. She puts up a wall, not to be difficult but to
protect her heart from those who don't deserve it. She hears the
compliments, but what she sees in the mirror is different from their
opinions. She struggles with the idea of being alone as if she'll
remain that way forever. She is you, fighting to confront the truth.
She is still trying, refusing to give up on the idea of real love. She
is good enough even when others overlook her. She is strong even
in a moment of weakness. She is intelligent and brave. She is both
unafraid of the fire and made up of flames that turn into a beautiful
ember. She's worth it, and anyone mature enough to realize her

worth will be worthy of her love. She knows that this was written about her.

She's not a bitch. She's just been through a few things, seen a few things, been there, and done that. She may be a little cold, but only because she once gave a damn about someone who failed to give a damn about her. She's built a fortress to protect her heart from further damage. You told her that you were different, but she won't believe it until you prove it. Words don't mean a thing; actions are everything. So, don't hold it against her for refusing to easily believe the words that fall from your mouth; do not misjudge her or label her out of laziness and or a refusal to truly put forth the effort it will take to prove yourself worthy of the love she's capable of sharing. She owes you nothing. She's built that wall in front of her heart, not to be difficult but to put separation between herself and anyone who may attempt to hurt her, and there's nothing wrong with that.

Sadly, the fear pushes us closer to everything we never wanted. We do the opposite of what we claimed we'd do given the situation. It's not like we've lost any brain cells or the ability to do better. The love we feel tends to blur things a bit, and that skill of decision-making begins to malfunction. We don't want to feel pain, but being alone is scary, so we decide to stay with the wrong person. You fool yourself into believing that having anyone is better than having no one, but you don't even realize that staying with the wrong person keeps you from finding a love worth holding on to.

do not deny your heartache
just to make others comfortable
do not shrink yourself
for the sake of satisfying others

I know it's not easy, saying goodbye to someone your heart wants to cling to, but don't let your love for that person blur the lines they've crossed when they betrayed you.

At 5:35am.

All you could say was "sorry," but apologies are often expressed by those who do not take the time to consider the feelings of the person they will hurt. We all know right from wrong, and what you're telling me is that you believe that I should forgive you because you mustered up the courage to say "sorry." Fuck, I just wish you were brave enough to love me properly. I wish it didn't take me getting hurt for you to understand my value.

A note for the weary.

What they won't tell you is that the end is not the end. And often, the relationship that stops working is more so a lesson and not the tragedy you may believe it to be. Most of what ends becomes a stepping-stone, a bridge to elsewhere, something better, if you're lucky. And if you don't find what you're looking for this next time around, you gain more insight into what to avoid going forward. You see, when one relationship ends, there's a moment in the time provided to know yourself further. The ending brings you to a path of self-love and rediscovery. If this relationship isn't supporting your happiness, I hope it ends. I hope you walk away so that you can find yourself again.

Between both ends.

I saw it in your eyes, the way you hesitated. You were suddenly
tasked with this decision to make, and I was tired of being forced to
share in this misery of believing that maybe I wasn't good enough,
but that pause, those 10 seconds that felt more like infinity. That
moment told me everything I needed to know. If I'm not the first
choice—the only option—then I don't want to be chosen, and if
you're confused about what you feel for me, let me go.

You can't control the other person; you can't force them to be who you deserve, but you can create an exit out of their life. You are capable of moving on without them.

More than ever, you are responsible for your peace of mind. If someone brings chaos into your life, you are allowed to refuse to accept it.

Don't just experience heartache; learn from it. See the lessons in every ounce you experience. Your exes, the ones who hurt you, teach you what to avoid. The family members who betray you are only teaching you what and who to walk away from, and any friend who abandons you will help you discover just how strong you've always been as you not only endure the pain but also learn to live without the wrong people.

You are under no obligation to share yourself with someone who would rather keep you hidden like a shameful secret.

real love is wrapped in truth
and kept warm with devotion and loyalty
and so, when they lie to you, leave you in the cold
while betraying you to be with someone else
please, understand that this is not love

You paint over the word "hate" to make it all seem beautiful because you love a person who will never be right for you, no matter how hard you try. You can't plant seeds of hope and devotion into the soil of a soul that doesn't intend to love you.

You were always so cold to me, but no matter how bad it got, summer always came, and this reminded me that you didn't have the power you thought you did. Life goes on, and so did I.

Eventually, it got too heavy, and we became too quiet. We stopped doing the things we used to do, and, shortly after, the words we once spoke were no longer said. Before you know it, everything becomes nothing.

You move on, not because you've forgotten about the pain. You move forward without that person because you're tired of getting hurt.

I'll be gone.

i saw a river burning
my mind began churning
turning my gaze toward you

once cleansed by your touch
my heart has caught fire
who knew you'd burn me

i sought heaven
but hell was near
what type of love
turns to dust

the type of love
you promised
but that sentiment
was just a lie

all the other times
i'd try
but this time
i'll leave

Today, I don't miss you as much as I did before. It's almost as if each moment is a step on a stairway toward everything you couldn't be and all the things I knew I wanted but was too afraid to go after. I felt stuck for quite some time, telling myself lies. I was fighting to find every excuse to stay here in this space of confusion. Oh, the years I've wasted on the idea of things getting better all while you grew comfortable with hurting my heart.

Now made nothing.

strong like sadness
beneath a full moon
on a winter's night
growing gray
like rain clouds
filled with gloom

consumed by my memories of you
running around, pacing heavily
but i still feel like i can't move

the most i could say was nothing
my silence the sound of bombs
whispers fading into every corner
our love reduced to hate
see, how lovers become enemies
feeling everything we could feel
until there was nothing left

how do you fix your lips
to say " i love you"
when you're the reason
i'm in hell

being alone with you
was the loneliest
i'd ever been

there is nothing to love
about a person who leaves you
to fuck someone else
then returns to say, "i miss you"

the heart should never feel guilt
for deciding to start over with someone better

You changed because you needed to be someone different. Your evolution, inspired by a pain you never wanted to feel, and so here you are, being someone you thought you couldn't be. Brave enough to love yourself despite the heartache of being neglected and overlooked by the person you cared about. Displaying the courage to envision a life alone without the person you thought you needed. And I hope you find the clarity to see which path you should take. Change is good, especially if it means you get another chance at real love, peace of mind, and joy.

I know how lonely it feels to be with the wrong person. I know how weary one can get when dealing with toxic family members. I know how painful it can feel when a friend stabs you in the back. I've known the everyday emptiness of working at a job I didn't enjoy. And I know that it all gets better over time. You just have to make more room for the things you enjoy. Make more space for the right people to enter your life. You just have to love yourself a little bit more so that you can find the courage to walk in the opposite direction of all the things that just hurt you. Give yourself the time you'll need in order to break free.

I burned that bridge because I knew you wouldn't swim to me; that way, whenever you decided to pretend to miss me, you'd have no way to reach my heart.

it must be painful to get your calls ignored
throughout the day
and only be called upon
after midnight
neglecting meaningful moments
for meaningless sex
starving your heart
to feed the body

Fuck closure.

you wanted closure
i needed it to be over
you wanted to try again
but i needed to leave you
to forgive you

i'm past all the empty promises
i built hope on your lies
you want another chance
but the first time, you barely tried

i think back to how it was
comparing it now
claims of love
then came the yelling
and now we communicate
without sound

there's no more love to give
no more promises to make
i'm empty, numb because of you
there's nothing left for you to take

I think that relationship ended so that you could have more time to create something beautiful within yourself. With time, you figure out how to transform the heartache into a bed of roses. The absence of that person hurts for a while, but then you discover that peace is capable of thriving when you've separated from the one person who should have loved you but chose to break your heart. And, of course, there will be moments when you'll experience some desire to reconnect with that person, but it's essential to respect the love you've cultivated in place of all the pain you used to feel. When a relationship ends, it's an opportunity to begin again, to start better with someone who will treat you with respect and love you know you deserve.

You take mountains and transform them into inspiration. You see obstacles, but you find a way. When life feels like hell, you skip through the flames in pursuit of everything you want and deserve. So, keep going.

I think you're trying your hardest to confront an inconvenient truth.
You've invested so much of yourself into this particular relationship
because you believed that you'd finally found someone to keep.
Weary from starting over time and time again, you thought you'd
found a resting place. But maybe this time this person is just a
lesson. A moment to learn what you do or don't want. Though these
relationships end and these sorts of people hurt you, maybe this
needs to happen so that you can finally realize what type of love
you deserve. And once you experience a relationship that is far less
than what you expected, you'll be able to walk away sooner the next
time because you'll know what to watch out for.

you haven't been okay for a while
you're honest about it
even when you don't speak
your eyes scream out in agony
restless through the night
you drag yourself to the next morning
watching the sun replace the moon

the promises are not
the only thing to get broken
the person who believed them
begins to crack just the same

what is clarity, seeing you change
become more of who you said
you could never be
doing things you claimed
you'd never do
what is closure, seeing you choose
the other person, the one who you told me
to never worry about

i wasn't insecure; i was never crazy
i saw through your lies
and somehow pretended
that you were telling the truth

you have to be brave
even when it scares you
have courage
even in doubt

you are meant for more
there is peace in your future
and to get there
you'll need to leave
some things behind

bad things do happen
but something good is coming
because something good
is what you deserve
and you are brave enough
to fight for it

I want to tell you the truth, something that your friends may not have told you, and maybe this truth will hurt a bit but also it may help you move on. It's not that he struggled to care for you; it's not that he didn't know how to protect your heart. Sometimes the guy you want more than anything just wants one thing from you and refuses to try after he's gotten what he wanted to begin with. He didn't struggle to love you; he didn't want to, and he never planned to. And even though this shit hurts, it's his loss, even if he fails to realize it. So, cry, as much as you need to; break down so that you can build yourself up and endure the storm that may come just so that you can understand how powerful you truly are.

_____

Do not force your forevers into someone who should stay an ex. Do not dream of a future with someone who should be left behind.

You've been shrinking yourself to make room for someone who will never deserve that space in your life, and this is why you feel so lost. Losing yourself to keep a person who rarely treats you like a person, and I hope you're reading this right now. I hope you find something here that reminds you to let go.

your absence is suffocating
your presence is suffocating
please stay; please go

Every now and then, you're going to come upon situations that will tempt you to fall apart. You will come face-to-face with people who will attempt to break you down. You will stand toe to toe with the resistance, roadblocks, and obstacles. And even when you stumble, you will find a way to keep fighting through whatever or whoever wants to hold you back. You have always been a warrior, and sometimes it takes a war to reveal this truth.

I learned that you should never be with a person who causes your mind to be at war with your heart.

———————————————

you were a stupid kind of clever
the way you fooled me into believing in you

---

you claimed to love me
but i just wish that love
was enough to keep you loyal

Just because they've taken up residence in your heart doesn't mean
they should remain in your life. You have to understand something.
When the heart genuinely cares, it may hold on to that person
longer than it should, but in no way should you continue to give
your love to anyone who has decided to break your heart repeatedly.

People leave, and they unintentionally provide space for someone better to walk into your life.

Beautiful heat.

you start fires
but not to hurt anyone
you start fires
to feel at home
because you are a flame
an everlasting blaze of glory
and strength and courage

we all see the rose
some will focus on its thorns
and others will wait
to see it bloom

i want to see you blossom

I knew I'd fall in love with you. I saw all the lines where your heart had been fractured and knew that I was staring at a woman who knew what it truly meant to survive. Within your soul lies the truth, the answers to all the questions I've had for years. The ones involving my future, a reason to leave behind the things of my past. You are the sum of all the pain I've experienced, the reward for letting go of everything that could no longer live in my life. And I'd like the chance to prove myself worthy. I'd like the opportunity to give, to show, to put on display my feelings for you. So, hear my song amid the chaos. I stand here in the rain, unafraid of storms or anything that would keep me away from you.

I've been waiting, craving the sweet devotion in your presence. And you, weary from the troubles of tainted love. Separate journeys down two entirely different paths, and somehow we meet in the middle. Cold and afraid while hoping for warmth against winter. Despite mountains in the way and distractions in the form of people, I knew all along that I would one day find you. I'm well aware that keeping the thing you discover has been the most challenging part, so I promise to give you a reason to stay.

i cast my hopes
to a winter's moon
i close my eyes
to see you soon

in a moment's time
i'll see your face
i'm coming home
i'll leave this place

———————————

you love him
you just don't like
the way it feels
when you're with him

Give yourself compassion and time.

———————————————

No need to climb or move mountains when you are capable of destroying them.

Look how willing we are to feast on lies when our heart has been
starved of connection.

Loving someone through their sadness can be difficult. Finding someone to love you through your sadness is even harder.

The ground beneath your feet began to crumble; this was when you discovered you could fly.

Give it back to yourself. All the time, the energy and love.

—————————————————

You can like the company of others and still love being alone.

Even on your darkest of days, you are still someone else's reason to survive. Remember this when you feel like giving up.

Say no more often. Saying no will give you the chance to say yes to the right things.

Someday it'll end and you will the find the courage to love again; start with yourself.

we never know the value of fire
until winter has come
and darkness silences the light

———————————————

Tell every obstacle to get the fuck out of your way!

---

broken heart
give it love
give it time

some people are in fact
difficult to get over
and this is why
you have to choose
to get through them
treat them like a door
not a mountain

I still believe that relationships are like flowers, and when they die, you're given the opportunity to grow differently, stronger.

Enduring heartbreak makes you stronger; as you grieve, you truly discover the value of peace, and when someone enters your life with the intent to destroy it, you learn just how important peace of mind really is. So much of what I've learned about love over the years came at the expense of my life and really challenged my ability to move forward and start over. One brush with a relationship that hurts you creates this fear of doing it all over again, and it's fucked up that we only discover the truth, the lies when we've given just about all that we can give. But if you can find a way to endure, to hold on, to continue to make excuses for why you're with the wrong person, then you can also open your fucking eyes and realize that you can and will survive being alone. I believe that being alone is the beginning of finding the right person to bring into your life.

Life is always teaching us things, and when you realize that you are to remain a student, you'll discover lessons in every moment. I met someone long ago, and in time that person revealed themselves as a foe. My rose-colored glassed reimagined everything that was happening at the time. I forced myself to believe that these were mistakes; the choices that this person decided to make were often in an attempt to hurt me. And, somehow, every time I thought about leaving, I felt guilty. You know that feeling. You feel leaving means quitting, and so you tell yourself that you're not the type of person to easily give up while the person you cling to has no issue with hurting your heart. You go from fighting beside one another to fighting against one another and fighting yourself over the decision to walk away. But I am thankful for all that went wrong; it showed me how to get it right. I am grateful for all the love that turned out to be tainted because now I can decipher the lie from the truth. Right now, this may be happening to you. As you read the words on this page, you may be struggling with these lessons in your own life. I think that's why you're reading this now; you're in search of an answer or a way out. Consider this for a moment: to find strength, you must sometimes get lost in a forest of anguish. And to be more sure, sometimes you must face the uncertainty of loving a person. I know it hurts now—the confusion of it all has weighed heavily on your mind—but you will find a way forward, a path that keeps you moving toward the things that'll fill your life with peace. These moments, these toxic relationships, are only temporary and can feel extended due to our inability to walk away. So, take the time to decide where you're going by understanding what you're leaving behind. Keep in mind that the thing you're leaving was just a key to open up an exit that will lead you to another door, and once that opens, you'll find your way back to yourself. Remember to mourn; take time to express your emotional truths. Do not hide behind a smile; do not lie about how you feel. Be truthful in your grief. Feelings can only linger when you suppress them; don't.

Andrews McMeel Publishing
a division of Andrews McMeel Universal
1130 Walnut Street, Kansas City, Missouri 64106

www.andrewsmcmeel.com

22 23 24 25 26 SDB 10 9 8 7 6 5 4 3 2 1

ISBN: 978-1-5248-7113-0

Library of Congress Control Number: 2022936532

Editor: Patty Rice
Art Director/Designer: Diane Marsh
Production Editor: Elizabeth A. Garcia
Production Managers: Cliff Koehler and Julie Skalla

ATTENTION: SCHOOLS AND BUSINESSES
Andrews McMeel books are available at quantity
discounts with bulk purchase for educational, business,
or sales promotional use. For information, please
e-mail the Andrews McMeel Publishing Special Sales
Department:specialsales@amuniversal.com.